FART
YOGA

Coloring Book
FOR ADULTS

I'M DOWN, DOG!

One day
this pain
will
make
sense to you.

c'mon,
inner peace.

I don't have
all day.

I'm down,
dog.

*** Bonus ***

The Subtle Art of Coloring with Love

ISBN: 978-1091160583

BONUS

Jeez Louise
The Most Innocent
Swear Word Coloring Book for Adults

ISBN: 978-1549759710

Made in the USA
San Bernardino, CA
07 June 2019